THE DOOR WAS NEVER LOCKED

REMEMBER WHAT YOU ARE

SAM SMITH

Field Notes from the Edge

Subscribe and I'll send you a private recording of me reading my favourite chapters:

about the author

I'm Sam. At the time of writing this, I'm thirty-five. I live in Bristol, UK, with my two boys, my wife Holly and our slightly old and lovely dog, Kobe.

I've lived a few lives already. I was a professional rugby player, with Harlequins, before retiring injured at twenty-six. I founded, built and lost a multi-million pound business. I almost erased myself with drugs and alcohol.

I've separated from the mother of my boys and together we've created a loving co-parenting relationship. I'm living a life with Holly, Freddie and Nelson that quite honestly blows my mind sometimes. Today, I am the peace I was searching for the whole time.

My work with clients often starts when people come to me with some kind of problem or need: stale relationships, loss of meaning, hollow successes, stuck-ness in business and life. That kind of thing.

But nothing we do together is about 'fixing'. Instead, I ask the only question that really matters – do you feel totally alive? I walk with them while they discover the freedom to be fully themselves, to be fully alive, often for the first time in their life.

I've partnered with artists, musicians, mums, authors, seekers, Olympians, CEOs, dads, students, founders and leaders. What happens in the space we create is magic.

THE DOOR WAS NEVER LOCKED
remember what you are

First edition 2025

Published by This Is The Changing Room Limited
www.thisisthechangingroom.com

ISBN: 978-1-9193952-3-4
Designed by Chloe Fuell
Edited by Nick Parker

disclaimer

This book shares reflections and lived experiences. It is offered for contemplation, not instruction. Nothing here is intended as medical, psychological, financial or professional advice. Each reader remains responsible for their own choices, interpretations and wellbeing. The names and identifying details of individuals have been changed in some cases to protect privacy.

Life shows you what you’re meant to see,
when you’re meant to see it.

For my world:
Holly, Freddie, Nel
& the little ones still to come

an opening

This book started to take shape during a period when I began to really see life for what it is. These ideas were alive. I was hearing them in real time, and my whole life began transforming around me.

It didn't feel like I even had much say in the matter— things just started happening. This book is my attempt to capture what I was experiencing in the moment.

These insights aren't guidelines, they aren't rules, and I don't always even understand where they came from or what they mean. They are bigger than me, and yet I know that they are me.

They point to what I had spent many years searching for — a search that I no longer feel the need to be engaged with, because what once felt impossible to understand now feels beautifully obvious.

It wasn't always this way.

When I was in the depths of the darkest period of my life in 2018, I started working with a wonderful man named Huw Richards. When I showed up at his studio for the first time, I was hungover, ashamed of who I had become.

Life changed fast working with Huw, and when I shared my disbelief with him about how that had even been possible, he said something that I'll never forget:

'Just because we have complicated locks, doesn't mean we need complicated keys.'

This book is an offering of simple keys to the doors you've been walking past your whole life, to remember what you are.

1 | the truth about peanut butter

For me, bread was invented
as an edible spoon
to transfer peanut butter into my body.

For my wife, Holly,
peanut butter should be kept for emergencies—
like plugging a leaky pipe
while you wait for the plumber.

Both of us are right.
Opposing truths can live side by side,
in harmony,
and both remain true.

The world has forgotten this.
It is obsessed with being right,
with proving,
with converting.

There is a universe available
where truth isn't up for debate.

It's a tool
for creating the life
you were always meant to live.

The truth is pure.
It speaks for itself.
It has impeccable timing.

Landing—
exactly where it's meant to,
exactly when it's meant to.

You'll know it when you feel it.

And in that knowing,
you can step over the threshold.

2 | you can only ever know what to do in the moment

Life shows you what you're meant to see,
when you're meant to see it.

You always have enough information in the moment.

When more is required,
life brings it—
an insight,
a question,
an illness,
a teacher.

Whatever we're shown to do,
it's always perfect.
You can only ever know what to do in the moment.

And knowing what to do in the moment
is all you'll ever need.

3 | borrowing your brother's trainers

A life lived from anything other than the truth
is not your life.

Like borrowing your older brother's trainers—
you'll certainly move,
you'll get places.
But they'll never fit.

A life built from truth
feels like your skin fitting you
for the first time.

You'll know it when you feel it.

Close your eyes right now,
ask yourself,
am I living from truth?

Your body will tell you.
And then you'll know what to do.

4 | your incompleteness is your completeness

Mum being ill
enabled me
to sense the energy of a whole household
before I'd finished
opening the front door as I returned from school.

Retiring from rugby at twenty-six
enabled me
to face my own darkness.

Battling with drugs and alcohol
enabled me
to find the peace
I'd always longed for.

Once upon a time
these stories were my trauma,
my suffering,
my sob story.

But because of these moments, I can:

Read the energy
of someone in seconds.

Hold someone's hand
as they face their own darkness
and not turn away.

Know, for a fact,
that the person sitting in front of me
has access
to their own peace.

My gifts were born
out of my incompleteness.

Knowing what I know now,
I would choose to go through all of it again.

When you see
that your incompleteness
is your completeness—
you are whole.

5 | thoughts are invitations you don't have to say yes to

Thoughts come in, broadcast
from somewhere outside us.

Like invitations to a party
that we know we don't want to attend,
because we've been before,
and the canapés sucked.

It was news to me when I learnt
that we don't have to say yes
to every invitation that pops into our head.

Welcome news, in fact.

My Party Invite Autoresponder had been set to 'yes'
for as long as I could remember.

I was in regular attendance at
the 'what if...' party,
the 'you're going to lose everything' ball,
and the 'you don't know what you're doing' shindig.

You can't dictate which invites are sent your way,
but you can choose which ones you say yes to.

But if you keep saying no
to the same invites again and again,
slowly the invitations start to lessen.

Thoughts are just invitations.
Nothing more.
You choose which parties to go to.

So, say 'no' to the next invitation.
And notice what happens in your body
when you politely decline.

6 | honour who got you here

It made sense,
once upon a time,
to become who you became.

And who you became
brought you here.

Don't make the old you wrong.

Stop fighting yourself.

Love who you've been.
Declare who you are.

You cannot be free
until you see that every step
has been perfectly trodden.

7 | judgement is a mirror

Most of the time
what looks like judgement of another
has everything to do with us.

We spot in someone else
a part of ourselves
we haven't yet learnt
to meet with compassion.

Other times, we're longing for a quality
we don't yet feel permission
to live.

I've watched this in myself.

I used to burst with road rage,
furious at the 'selfish twat'
who cut me up.

Yet if I hadn't been stuck in judgement,
I might have wondered
'were they just late
for the dentist?'

I used to judge other parents
as strict, uptight, controlling –
until I admitted
how hard boundaries felt
in my own parenting.

None of this means
that other people's behaviour
never crosses a line.

Discernment matters.

Boundaries matter.

But judgement often carries news
about our inner world
more than it does
about the person in front of us.

And when someone judges you,
it likely has nothing to do with you,
and everything to do
with their own view of themselves.

Not always.

But often enough
that it's worth remembering.

8 | stories are prisons, questions are keys

The context to your problems
isn't necessary.

It's you
enrolling yourself and others
into the web
of your made-up story.

It's much better
to ask questions
that open fresh pathways
into the future—
than wrestle
with the stories
you think brought you
to this place.

Stories are prisons.
Questions are keys.

9 | the infinite hunger of need

Living from need
is what most of us do,
most of the time.

But there is never enough
to satisfy the infinite hunger of need.

When you say,
'I need...'
what you are really saying is,
'I am not whole.'

I've done this plenty of times myself.

Hiring coaches
because I thought I needed their support
to step into the next phase of my life.

Only to realise
that we had partnered
to draw out what was already present within me.

Don't rob yourself of wholeness.
Trade need for want
and find yourself expanding inwards.

10 | everyone experiences life as it occurs to them

You are never experiencing
life in the same way
as the person
standing next to you.

When you see that,
you'll see life
for what it truly is.

11 | stop fishing

Humans love to get attached.
Attached to an outcome.
Wishing this moment were different.
Believing life should be otherwise.

We are like obsessed fishermen.
Casting, hooking, reeling—
over and over and over,
believing the next fish will be the one.

Notice when you're fishing.
Put the rod down.
Sit back.
Leave the fish.
Enjoy the gentle rocking of the boat.

Freedom isn't never fishing.
It's knowing you can always put the rod down.

12 | shame burns in the light

Starve a candle of oxygen—
it ceases to be.

Starve your shame of darkness.
Bring it out of hiding.
Share it.

Watch it go out.
Just like that.

You might tremble.
Sweat through your fingertips.
Feel your stomach fold into origami.
That's okay.
All of it is okay.

Decades of suffering lift in a moment,
as a client shares their darkest, dirtiest truth with me.
The kind of truth they thought they could never speak.

Find someone who can hold you as you let go
and fall apart.
And they'll still be there when you look up
and realise that you are okay.

What you did or didn't do isn't the issue.

Shame isn't the issue.
Hiding it in the dark is.

13 | move your feet

A friend once said to me,
'Life has just dealt me
the worst hand ever.'

I asked him—
who decided
it was the worst hand ever?

He responded,
'Well, I did.'

Where you stand
determines what you experience.
You'll see all the evidence you need
to support where you are standing
as the truth.

'Would you like to go stand in 'this is the greatest hand ever' for a moment?'

He resisted.

We often do
when defending our truth.

Eventually he moved.
His whole being relaxed.
'This is the best I've felt in ages.'

I won't tell you what he saw.
What he saw doesn't matter.
What he felt did.

Move your feet.

14 | expressing what you already are

There can be no freedom
when you believe that something outside of you
will give you something.

Starting a business
in order to feel fulfilled.
Losing 10 kilos
in order to feel sexy.

At best, you'll feel relief when you get there.

I grew my coffee business
to multiple millions in revenue,
all in order to prove
I was good enough.

It was never enough.
And so long as I played that game,
I was never enough.

Instead, try doing something
'as an expression of...'

Starting a business
as an expression of your passion.
Losing 10 kilos
as an expression of love
toward your body.

You are already free
to express who you are.

15 | stop pretending that you wish it was easy

'I just want it to be easy.'

She meant it.
The last year in her business
had been full of challenges.

Until this question:
'How easy did you find your old job?'

'Ridiculously easy.'

'And was that a good thing?'

'No. I hated it.
It's why I left
to start my own business.'

The penny dropped.

Her shoulders relaxed,
stale air gently exhaling.

She looked up,
a grin on her face.

She got it.

16 | the notes and the silence

The warm cup of coffee in your hands.
The rain on the window.
The dog gently snoring.

This is it.
This moment.

You could be in an infinite number of places.
But you aren't.
You're here.

You were never meant
to be anywhere else.

When you see this,
a door opens.
A door to unfiltered aliveness.

Each scene in your life
is an essential part of your story.

What's more important in a song—
the notes or the silence?

17 | fear as a signpost

My fear of writing this book was real.

It was the fifth idea I've had for a book.
The first I've taken past one hundred words.

Signs you're about to step over:

Resistance.
Fear.
Procrastination.
Tears.
Curiosity.
Action.
Terror.
Joy.
Laughter.
Fascination.

Welcome to the threshold.
You are right on track.

18 | the kitchen sink test

Every time I am on the edge
of a breakthrough—
I feel like I am about to break.

Like life is throwing
the kitchen sink, the fridge, the whole house at me,
trying to scare me away
from stepping over the threshold
into a new beginning.

My mind goes haywire.
I feel like giving up.

This used to almost defeat me.
Now I know it's a sign
that I am on the edge
of something beautiful.

I keep going,
I let the kitchen sink whistle over my head
and side-step the fridge.
through the muck and the mess.

And I see
the first slivers of a new dawn.

19 | silence always shows you what to do

Notice when you get needy
and start asking others
for solutions.

Praying this person
will give you the answer.
Hoping they'll take responsibility
for your life.

Wishing you didn't have to face
the truth that's been knocking
inside you for months.

No answer to your question
can ever be found
outside of you.

Others can only prescribe
from their own experience.

And their experience
has nothing to do with you.

Find people in your life
who can sit with you
in silence,

until you know
exactly what to do.

20 | if nothing is true, choose what works

If life stops working—
or never quite got started—
take a look
at what you believe to be true.

The unworkability of your life
always rests
inside the truth you've chosen.

Pick a new truth.
One that makes possible
the experience you've been
looking for.

I once believed
I wasn't a leader.
I wasn't loud enough.
Charismatic enough.
Articulate enough.

And so I lived a life
picking up the crumbs
of others.

The day I decided the truth was:
quiet, calm, measured people
like me
can lead,
was the day
I became a leader.

The truth is always
waiting for you
to speak it.

21 | the peace of enough

'I am enough.
I have enough.'

I send these words
to my heart
each morning.

I declare them
to be the truth.

I have no proof for this.

Just like I never had proof
when I told myself
I wasn't good enough either.

22 | when love comes out to play

Unconditional love
gets a lot of air time.

Something to live up to.
Something to fall short of.

An infinite ideal,
just out of reach
of the finite human
searching for it.

Townsend Wardlaw gifted
a simpler way:

'You are either loving
or judging.'

Binary.

Notice judgement.
Choose love.

That's the practise.

Notice judgement.
Choose love.

Being loving isn't about loving more.
It's about judging less.

Less judgement.
More space.

And in that space,
the love you already are
comes out to play.

23 | commitment is the only plan

At the intersection
of certainty
and non-attachment
lives commitment.

Commit
to the seemingly impossible
with absolute certainty
that it will happen,
and total non-attachment
to how,
if,
or when it happens.

Do this,
and life steps in
to assist you.

Chance encounters.
Flashes of inspiration.
Phone calls from the blue.

Commit.
Trade doubt for certainty.
Lay attachments down.

When you commit,
life turns impossible into inevitable.

Commitment creates
the next step.
And the next step
is all you need.

There is no plan.
There is only commitment.

24 | words create worlds

You do not describe reality.
You create it.

Every word you speak,
think,
and write
is creation.

'I don't know'
becomes
'I am certain
that I am still working it out.'

'I failed'
becomes
'I learnt.'

'I wish I could'
becomes
'I know I can.'

What becomes available
depends on what you create.

Reality is always
a lagging indicator.

Empowered or disempowered.
You decide.

Before you speak,
ask yourself what world you want to create.

25 | what losing £100k taught me about questions

I had just lost £100,000
liquidating my company.

Newly separated,
raising my two sons,
thirty days
to pay the mortgage.

I started by asking myself:
'How is this possible?'
with only three coaching clients at the time.

A small-minded question,
splintering into a thousand noisy routes.
The kind of question
that creates more static
than clarity.

So I stepped into
a beautiful, powerful, expansive question:
'How can I cover
twelve months of mortgage payments
in the next thirty days?'

Within twelve hours,
I had my answer.

I created a coaching programme,
to be paid upfront,
that covered the whole year.

A day passed
and a new client sent me the money.

From noise to clarity,
the only thing that lay between them
was a different question.

If you want to live a miraculous life,
ask miraculous questions.

26 | using resentment to create a life that works

Expectations are what
those unwilling
to take responsibility for their life
hide behind.

Unspoken.
Undefined.
Cowardly.

Like expecting your partner to know
how tired you are,
how much you need
a night off bedtime.

And then, when they mention
they're heading to the gym,
you detonate—
silently—
in a cloud
of resentment.

Steve Chandler taught me about the power of agreements.

Notice resentment—
it's a sign that there is no agreement in place.
A chance to create more peace and freedom in your life.

Create an agreement
with someone you love.
Create an agreement
with your boss.
Create an agreement
with yourself.

Create them together.
Create mutual responsibility.
Create a life that works.

Expectations rot.
Agreements nourish.

27 | speaking the future into existence

Your life doesn't work
if you don't do
what you said
you would do.

You are either in integrity,
or you are not.

Integrity isn't about being good.
It's about being whole and complete.

For a car to be in integrity,
all its components must be working as intended.

The car must do what it says it will do.
If the windscreen wipers break,
it's out of integrity—
not wrong or bad,
just less effective.

Use action
to complete your word.
Know that when you say something
it gets done.

The more you practise,
the stronger your word becomes.

Notice when you're out of integrity
and clean it up.

The highest integrity we can hold
is picking back up what we dropped.

Without your word,
you're just noise.

When your word means something,
you can speak the future into existence.

28 | life only speaks into silence

A man dialled in from Indonesia
to our men's community call.

He spoke of how he'd given himself this break
in order to hit the ground running
when he got back.

Callum stopped him in his tracks.

Taking time off in order to be on again
is just more on-ness,
wrapped in a neat disguise.

In Peru on our honeymoon,
I was totally off.

And on the second morning,
as I lay in bed,
life plugged in the USB stick of inspiration
and downloaded the chapters of this book
directly into my brain.

Choose to be off
and watch the miracles
that find their way into your space.

Not because you asked for them.
But because you didn't.

29 | I only do what I want, and it always gets me what I want

Two hours with Gary Mahler.

He said,
'I only do what I want
and it always gets me what I want.'

This truth fizzed
with effervescent aliveness.

What you want
and what life wants
are the same thing.

And not what you think you want,
or think you should want.
What you madly,
deeply,
truly want.

When you give yourself to want,
life gives itself to you.

30 | whose rocks are in your rucksack

The world is full of people
wearily trudging through life
with heavy backpacks.

The heaviness feels like responsibility.
But so often, the backpacks
are simply full of rocks.

Your partner's mood is a rock.
Your child's future is a rock.
Your boss's opinion of you is a rock.

You cannot be responsible
for someone else's experience of life.

You can think you are.
You can tell people you are.
You can feel important:
'Look! I'm carrying all this weight!'

But it is not your job to save,
or fix, or improve
another human.

Their life is not yours to carry.

Carrying other people's rocks
is a way of avoiding responsibility
for your own life.

So, put down the rocks.

31 | you are allowed to be unreasonable

We're told
we must give a reason
for everything.

Justifying
our existence.

Asking permission
to be alive.

The freest people
do not give reasons.

They are free to want.
Because they want.

32 | the proof that you are limitless

If you want to expand,
find your edge.
Then step over it.

What felt impossible
becomes possible.

Play this game
for the rest of your life,
and know
that there is no edge
you cannot step over.

You are limitless.
But proof of your limitlessness
can only be found
at your edge.

33 | don't be a hard lifer

When you want life to be hard,
life obliges.

It'll be all you see.
All you experience.
All you speak about
with the other hard-lifers.

The easy life is here.
Waiting.

Ask yourself:
'If this was easy, what would I see?'
'If this was easy, what would I do?'

It's surprising how hard people find it
to ask themselves this question.

They're not ready
for life to be easy.

34 | you are already proven

Stepping onto a rugby pitch,
stuck in the infinite game
of proving.

Rarely free enough to play.

Until the moment
I signed a contract
to leave Harlequins.

Scoring five tries
in the final third
of the season.

Because I allowed myself
to have nothing left to prove.

Prompting my coach
to ask if I could stay.

Stop performing
for the crowd.
Start living
for yourself.

Proving is for the broken.
Expression is for the complete.

And no one is broken.

35 | fuelled by fear or love

I've worked with Olympians,
professional athletes,
and entrepreneurs.

All fuelled
by fear.

Fear can be rocket fuel.
Fear enables us to create works of art,
performances that take breath away,
companies that change the world.

If using fear to create success was an equation,
it'd look like this:

Tell myself I am not successful = I become successful

When this is your system,
and it works—
you will never allow yourself
to feel successful.

To feel successful
would break the system.

And so,
you stay hungry,
restless,
forever chasing.

There is another system.
Fuelled by love.

It works.
It's infinite.
And it feels good to use.

36 | life doesn't make mistakes

Welcome what's here,
even when you think you don't want it.

Watch it soften.
Thank it for showing up.
Feel it transform.

Ask to hear what it has to teach you.
Listen.

Life doesn't make mistakes.
What's here is here.

It couldn't be any other way.

There's always a message in the bottle.

37 | borrow someone else's eyes

At a retreat we closed
with an acknowledgement circle.

Eyes leaked,
hearts opened.

So rarely do we share with others
who they truly are to us.

What a waste,
to leave love unspoken.

If you could see yourself
through my eyes,
there could be no doubt
about what
and who you are.

Uncertainty would melt.
The voice inside your head
would quieten.

When in doubt,
borrow someone else's eyes.

38 | radio consciousness

Stood in a prep kitchen
when a phone call came in
that changed the rest of my life.

She told me
she was pregnant with Freddie.

We'd been together three months.

My whole body lit up,
every single cell rushed with energy.
My mind was screaming doubts.
My body knew what I needed to do.

You are connected
to infinite consciousness.
Direct dial—
signal always on.
Crystal clear wisdom
available at any moment.

Like an old-school radio, though,
you must tune in.

Twist the dial
to find radio consciousness.

Notice when you've tuned into static,
or stations like Fear FM
and Needy 100.

Come back to radio consciousness.

You could live the rest of your life
tuned into radio consciousness.
And it would be
the most beautiful thing
you could ever imagine.

If you want to live like this, though,
you'd have to put down
the idea that you know best.

Trust in signal.
Tune out noise.

39 | you are allowed to ask for help

What you want
is on the other side of asking for help.

And the moment you ask,
you realise you never needed it.

Ask anyway.

Not for the answer.

40 | find the competing commitment

If you say you want one thing,
but you have something else—
it's because you are more committed
to the something else.

You say you want a great relationship with your kids,
but you're more committed
to soothing the anxiety
that keeps you working late.

You say you want to be fit and healthy,
but you're more committed
to comfort.

You say you want to live your dreams,
but you're more committed
to staying safe.

We've all done this.

There is nothing wrong
with being committed to something else.

No commitment trumps another.
There is no good or bad.

But there is always a commitment.
And you get what you are committed to.

41 | once you get it, you don't get it

Every new piece of information—
'Ah yes, I get it!'

But as soon as you get it,
you no longer get it.

How could you truly
get anything?

Do you know how you love?
Do you know how you breathe?
Do you know how gravity works?

Realise you have absolutely no idea
about anything.

Love not knowing.
Not knowing
is knowing.

Stop trying to get it.
You'll start getting it.

42 | choose the future that changes you now

The way we are taught to set goals
– S.M.A.R.T! –
is like pulling on the hand break of your potential.

S hrink yourself
M eet expectations
A void risk
R epeat last year
T ry not to fail

Goals based on your current capabilities
just become
another to-do list.

Choose goals
so ridiculously crazy
the current version of you
could never make them happen.

This is how you create a future
that changes your now.

Impossible filters out all the noise.

Give DUMB goals a go:

D aring
U nrealistic
M agical
B old

Set goals not to achieve them,
but to explore what's possible,
to taste your infinite nature.

43 | where are you ending up?

What is it all for?

Where are you ending up?

44 | trying is the ultimate cop-out

'I'll give it a try.'

Life's ultimate cop-out.

Setting yourself up
to be okay
with the fact
you didn't do
what you said
you were going to do.

Life only responds
to what you do.

45 | value is an inside job

Working with
a brilliant executive—
best in the industry.

But he hadn't ever managed
to step into his own value.
To own it.

He reconnected
with his power, his truth—
and the people around him
started to notice.

Family members,
for the first time,
saw how incredible
his career had been.

Work asked him
to step up
and take on another department.

Life then put
his remembered self-worth
to the test.

In a session
we created the salary
he truly wanted.
And he committed
to standing firm in his value.

Only you get to decide your worth.

It's an inside job.

The first offer
was laughable.

An older version of him
would have said yes.
Swallowed the resentment.
Waited six months,
then left for pastures new.

Not this time.

He sat calm in the meetings,
refusing to accept
less than what he is worth.

He rejected two more offers.

Until finally
they caught up
to the value he had already created inside himself.

He got what he wanted—
a fourfold increase on
their original offer.

He never named the number.
He didn't need to.

You always get
what you decide you're worth.

46 | what you want and what life wants are the same

'What do I want from life?
What does life want from me?'

Neena Sims asked me to write them each
on a separate sheet of paper,
and lay them down in front of me.

I stood staring at them.

She walked over,
slid the sheets on top of one another,
and quietly invited,
'What if they're the same thing?'

If what we are
is consciousness aware of itself—
an infinite connection to source,
a wave on the ocean,
a grain of sand in the desert—
then our wants
must be life's wants for us.

The wave does not ask the ocean
for permission to rise.

The ocean does not love
one wave over another.

Want from truth,
and notice ease.

Want from the centre of your heart,
and remember:
it was never yours
in the first place.

47 | see where you're not, and stop

I watched Steve Hardison
coach my friend.

She asked him
how she could become more powerful.

'Simple,' he said,
'Notice all the places in your life
where you are being unpowerful.

And stop.'

48 | needing to be right is ludicrous

Needing to know you are right
before taking action
is like needing to know it's Tuesday
before making breakfast.

You are certain
you will eat breakfast.

So you make it.
You eat it.
You don't sweat it.

Why make it different
for the big stuff?

Who decides what's big anyway?

Treat every action
like a bowl of porridge—
and watch your world expand.

49 | it's either in the way or it is the way

There are two ways
to look at anything in life:

'This is in the way.'
'This is the way.'

Everything
is the way.

50 | there is no freedom from, only freedom with

Anyone selling you
freedom from something
cannot deliver.

There is no freedom
from anything.

The human experience
is a full-spectrum experience.

There is only
freedom with.

51 | possibility lives inside choice

When you have no choice,
remember there is always one.

Once there is choice,
possibility appears.

And possibility
is the essence of life.

52 | create from already successful

Are you creating your life
'in order to be successful'
or from
'I am already successful?'

Stand in both places.
Look out at your life.

Notice what you notice.

And choose the life
you want to live.

53 | letting awe in

Awe usually arrives
as a rare visitor.
A sudden shiver.

A few tears.
Then gone.

No forwarding address.
No hint of when it might return.

Lately it's been showing up
far more often.
The sun catching the disco ball
in our living room
at just the right time of day,
filling the room with stars.

Nelson — four years old —
remembering this morning
that snakes used to have legs,
something he learnt on safari
almost a year ago.

The vividness of life
when I'm actually engaged with it,
to the point where walking down a street
feels like I've wandered
into one of those slow, artsy films
that Holly loves so much.

What I'm noticing
is that awe isn't just a feeling
that arrives unannounced...
it's a side-effect
of paying attention.

54 | do you actually need to play a bigger game?

Do you need to 'go bigger'?
Or simply see
where you already are?

Ambition is a quiet thief.
It steals the present
and sells it back
as a future.

But everything real
is happening now —
here.
In the places
you keep walking past.

The biggest game
you could ever play
is the one
that doesn't need
to be played.

55 | do you want the coffee or the mug?

Be careful deciding
what you want.

A whole life can pass
chasing one thing,
hoping it will deliver another.

The mug will promise you coffee
if you stare at it long enough.
It's convincing.
Everyone else believes it too.

But coffee doesn't live in mugs.
It only passes through.

56 | what if you really were allowed to be yourself?

Children are so alive
because they aren't trying
to be anyone
other than who they were born to be.

Freddie and Nelson
can captivate a whole room
without even trying.

No effort,
only ease.

Step into the knowing
that you have permission.

See all the places in your life
where you can put down the act.

Lean back,
into your own skin.

Revealing the path
that's been patiently waiting for you.
The one only you can walk.

57 | you will only ever be given what you are ready for

Life constantly calibrates
against your capacity.

It will never send you
anything
you aren't ready for.

Know this—
and know that okay
is all you could ever be.

58 | never say never

I look forward to the day
when new truths arise.

When I read these pages
and smile lovingly
at the old me.

What a day that will be—
to discover treasures I had overlooked,
to see the familiar as strange,
the known as unknown.

The secret of the symphony
is that it never ends.

And isn't that fortunate?

Because what a tragedy it would be
to ever arrive
thinking you had it all figured out.

59 | this is your last conversation

If you knew this was your last conversation—
would you still play it safe?

Hold nothing back.
Empty yourself.

Let love pour out of you,
and watch life pour in.

Better to be spent,
than saved.

There is no later.

60 | play the game

We are in the most beautiful game.
The game of life.

The only reason to play
is to learn more about life.
To experience
your own uncensored aliveness.

There is no trophy.
Only your thumping heart.

acknowledgements

I have a lot of people in my life to thank. We cannot help but be shaped by those around us, especially the ones who take an interest and walk beside us whether it's for decades or a single conversation. These are some of my people. There are more and if you are not named, know that you live in my heart always.

When Huw Richards put his hand on my shoulder in my coffee shop and asked me to go for a coffee, I knew he wanted to help, and I wasn't ready to receive it. Thankfully, he was patient, and the rest is history. This man is special. I love him a lot, and I am so grateful that after all the help he gave me, I now get to call him my friend.

Rob Poynton's book 'Do Pause' was a big slosh of cold water to the face. He woke me up to a new way of living, and when he started Yellow with Alex Carabi, I fell deeper and deeper back into myself. Back into full permission to be myself. I'll never forget the week we spent walking in the mountains by his house in Spain. One of the most beautiful experiences of my life. A week that led directly to the life I live today.

Andy Rogers was my mentor during my coaching qualification with Thirdspace, but Andy did so much more than help me become a coach. As my relationship broke down, my business fell apart, and I embraced single parenting, Andy stepped up in a big way and held me in the most loving embrace for the remainder of that year. I will never forget it.

Neena Sims, also on faculty at Thirdspace, waited until the last thirty minutes of the year-long programme to blow my whole world open with a single question: 'What do you really want, Sam?' I collapsed into a pile of sobs, and when I sat back up my answer was simple: 'I want to be a kid again.' Neena then took my hand and walked with me for a year while I reconnected with the essence of myself. I love this wonderful woman a lot, and I know we'll be connected for life.

Douglas Sharp entered my life by pure serendipity. I met him at a mask workshop in London. He had flown down from Scotland for the day. Six months later, he became my therapist. The work we did together was intense, eighteen months of somatic therapy.

My interior is so spacious these days; it is a delight to exist within it. I have our work together to thank for this.

I had been in Townsend Wardlaw's orbit for eighteen months before I committed to ten hours working with him. And what a ten hours it was. Townsend models what becomes possible when you are able to sit with someone in silence, in the belief that they already have everything they could ever want. He helped me not only see that I am infinite, but guided me into it as a lived, embodied experience. I started writing this book toward the end of our time together and so much of what is in these pages I have Townsend to thank for. I know we have some seriously exciting adventures ahead of us.

Dyl Salamon is my best friend. Dyl, if you're reading this, I love you and I am forever grateful for the support you have always given me.

Nick Parker means a lot to me, he lives somewhere in the midst of friend, inspiration, client and the editor of this book. I met him at Rob's house in Spain and what we have experienced together since has been pretty nuts. Thank you for being in my life, for your kindness, believing in this project and in me. So much so you offered to help me edit this book, I quite literally could not have done it without you. You are such a gifted man and I am glad I get to experience that gifted-ness with you.

My mum and dad. I could write for days about you both. What I will say is this: I have such deep love and respect for you both. You have loved me completely since the day I was born and I know I would not be here writing this if I hadn't felt that deep down all along. You have always believed in every mad idea I have shown up with and in my eyes, belief is one of the greatest gifts you can give a child. So thank you for giving it to me.

To my siblings, George and Lizzie, thank you for always being here for me, two solid rocks of support in my life. I love how close we've become in the last few years and I am always here for you both too.

To my two little boys, Freddie and Nelson — you guys rock. I love you both so much. Finding out I was going to be your dad was the best news I had ever received, and it lit the fire that led to so much of what is in these pages. I learn so much about being alive from watching you exist and I am so excited that I get to be your dad for the rest of my life.

When I started dating again, I had this idea that I would not find someone who would love and accept me as a single parent. I thought at best they might tolerate it. Then I met Holly, and I knew instantly that I was wrong. I fell in love with her from our very first FaceTime, where she was interviewing me to see if I was worth dedicating an evening of her time to. I passed, and it was lucky she checked, because our first date lasted nine hours.

Holly sees me, loves me and holds me like no other. The fact I get to live the rest of my life with her is so great that I can't even put it into words. The world is better for Holly being in it, especially mine and the boys' world. The way she is with them blows me away. So much love and joy are brought into this home of ours. Watching their relationships deepen and grow is a privilege. These days, if anyone asks who my coach is, my response is Holly.

Thank you for listening, for nudging and for letting me read this book to you about 308 times. I love you.

a note from sam

Thank you for taking the time to be with and experience this book.

If you ever want to be in touch
or continue a conversation that's opening in you,
you can find me here:

sam@thisisthechangingroom.com

With love,

Sam

If something in these pages spoke to you,
an honest review helps others find the book:

Printed in Great Britain
by Amazon

da8fe598-c3b3-40d8-b729-01ba862a610aR01